E. M. Longhurst

VICTORIAN FURNITURE

Frontispiece. Cabinet and Stand of ebony with gilt metal mounts and Wedgwood plaques. The large porcelain plaque is a copy, by George Gray, of Mulready's 'Crossing the Brook'. The cabinet was designed by Professor Gottfried Semper and made by Holland & Sons for the 1855 Paris Exhibition. *Victoria and Albert Museum.*

VICTORIAN FURNITURE

Simon Jervis
Victoria and Albert Museum

WARD LOCK & CO. LIMITED
London and Sydney

Published by
Ward Lock & Co. Limited
116 Baker Street, London W.1

Printed in Great Britain by
Cox and Wyman Ltd.
Reading

Set in Monotype Imprint

ACKNOWLEDGMENTS

The colour photograph of one of the State Apartments of Osborne House illustrated on the jacket is reproduced by courtesy of the Ministry of Public Building and Works, and the monochrome photograph of the Chevy Chase sideboard by courtesy of Trust Houses Ltd.

INTRODUCTION

In 1780 the population of this country was seven and a half millions; by 1850 it had increased to eighteen millions. This expansion went hand in hand with the Industrial Revolution and the rise of a middle class totally different both in size and character from that which had existed in the eighteenth century. These facts are basic to an understanding of the history of the development of furniture in the last century. The growth of the middle class and the explosion in the population of provincial towns produced a situation in which a small London-based group of rich and, for the most part, aristocratic dilettanti and their talented protégés could no longer create fashions which would be accepted by the country as a whole. The traditional organization of the furniture trade was unfitted to cater for a vastly increased market; new manufacturing techniques, new materials and new methods of production had to be developed. Even if a consensus of taste had existed in the early nineteenth century, the pressures of such a situation would probably have caused a crisis. However, far from such a consensus existing, individualism and eclecticism were essential qualities of the romantic movement which dominated taste at this period. These conditions provided ideal opportunities for the self-expression of genius, but their effect on the manufacturers of furniture and their middle-class clients was disastrous. This lack of a secure basis of tradition was responsible for the struggles which continued throughout the century between conservatives, who searched for such a basis, and progressives, who tried to create a new tradition. Their efforts to create a style without stable foundations give Victorian furniture much of its fascination.

In the 1820s the classical purity which was the aim of the most distinguished designers of the Regency period became coarsened. C. H. Tatham (*Examples of Grecian and Roman Architectural Ornament*, 1799) and Thomas Hope (*Household Furniture and Interior Decoration*, 1807) had provided patterns for imitation which were based on strictly archaeological

5

researches into surviving examples and illustrations of ancient furniture. Their ideas, together with those of contemporary French archaeologists and designers, were popularized and domesticated by commercial designers such as George Smith (*A Collection of Designs for Household Furniture and Interior Decoration*, 1808). The robust, elegant and practical furniture of this period was followed by an increasing tendency towards grandiose over-ornamentation and clumsiness, typified by Michelangelo Nicholson's designs (*The Practical Cabinet Maker*, 1826). This debased Regency style, called 'Grecian' or 'Antique' by the early Victorians, was one of the basic furniture styles until about 1855. At its best the 'Grecian' style has a certain sobriety and solidity far less objectionable than many contemporary excesses. The important firm of Gillows continued to make furniture in this conservative style until well into the second half of the century. Architects, among them Philip Hardwick, Charles Barry and Henry Whitaker, often designed 'Grecian' furniture; the latter's 1844 designs for the Conservative Club are typical.

From about 1825 onwards a revival of the curvilinear Louis XV style took place. The Elizabeth Salon at Belvoir Castle decorated with Louis XV boiseries and furniture by Matthew Wyatt at this date was among the earliest examples; inaccurately this type of decoration was known as 'Louis XIV'. Writers of the period were unanimous in condemning this revival; it was French at a time when the tendency was towards purely English styles and its rococo lightness and elegance appeared frivolous to serious architects and designers. Despite critical disapproval the style enjoyed a great measure of success, especially for drawing-rooms and boudoirs; it satisfied the Victorian desire for display and the curving scrolls, which are its hallmark, could be applied indiscriminately to all types of furniture without any deep knowledge of design. Another powerful factor in favour of its adoption was the popularity of the 'Louis XIV' in France; French design was much admired, and envied, by manufacturers and had a great influence on commercial design. An offshoot of 'Louis XIV' was the first original discovery of the Victorian age, the 'naturalistic' style. Characterized by opulent curves, naturalistic carving and swelling mounds of upholstery, this encouraged the use of original forms of an almost abstract plasticity. It was not, however, an officially recognized style and was propagated not by designers and architects but by mainly anonymous trade catalogues and pattern books. The result was that designs tended towards indiscipline and amorphousness. 'Mixed' was a derogatory epithet frequently applied to this type of furniture by contemporary critics; they were concerned at the way in which decorative elements borrowed from other styles and naturalistic carving were frequently combined on a piece of original form. Like the 'Louis XIV' the style flourished among manufacturers; its exuberance and reassuring rotundity clearly appealed to those who valued comfort above dignity and had no sense of their duty to live in respectably historicist surroundings. The 'naturalistic' style appealed to the uninformed and symbolized to reformers a lowest common denominator of public taste; even today it seems the most essentially Victorian of Victorian styles.

While both the 'Louis XIV' and 'naturalistic' styles were either frowned upon or ignored by serious critics, the 'Elizabethan' style was approved and encouraged. The novels of Sir Walter Scott played a large part in bringing about a revival of interest in this period and his Scottish baronial home, Abbotsford, was one of the earliest houses to be decorated, in parts at least, in the Elizabethan style. Another strong influence was the publication in 1836 of Henry Shaw's *Specimens of Ancient Furniture*; Shaw illustrated a series of pieces ranging from Gothic to Restoration, nearly all of English manufacture. A national style was thus provided untainted by the frivolity of the detested eighteenth century. Furthermore it was basically a renaissance style and could therefore be adopted by those who disliked the Gothic as much as the Grecian. The adjective 'Elizabethan', as with so many Victorian descriptions of earlier furniture, is inaccurate. With little regard for historical consistency, the style borrowed from English furniture from Henry VIII to Charles II and, where sophistication was lacking in the native product, from foreign examples of the period. With Gothic, Elizabethan was recommended in 1835 as a suitable style for the rebuilding of the Palace of Westminster and thus officially recognized as a national style. However, although writers paid it lip-service, the style received little of the passionate loyalty accorded to Gothic. The architect Anthony Salvin designed Elizabethan furniture, which was also quite popular for commercial purposes. But its inherent eclecticism, combined with an almost complete lack of accuracy in its application, resulted in its becoming no more than a patriotic equivalent of the naturalistic style; in fact the two often overlapped in the same piece of furniture.

Of the historicist styles so far discussed Grecian was a final devitalized expression of the cult of antiquity which had dominated the arts since the Renaissance; while Louis XIV and Elizabethan were recent revivals of styles which were ill-understood by the Victorians and unsuited to provide an all-inclusive system of ornament. Gothic suffered from none of these faults. Horace Walpole's rococo Strawberry Hill and William Beckford's sublime Fonthill were much mocked by Victorians but they had stirred interest in a national style which had been neglected since the early sixteenth century. Romantic literature further re-awakened interest and antiquarian researches provided a corpus of accurate drawings which could be used by architects and designers. A vigorous programme of church

7

building, Catholic Emancipation and the growth of the Tractarian movement all contributed to the vitality of the revival. A further asset was the presiding influence of A. W. Pugin, whose reforming zeal affected everyone, even if it exasperated some. In the 1820s his father, A. C. Pugin, published a book entitled *Gothic Furniture*; it contained designs which were unsound both functionally and archaeologically; crockets, gables, tracery and pinnacles were applied superficially and indiscriminately to furniture forms which were either basically Regency or purely fanciful. His son's earlier designs were in the Regency 'Gothick' tradition but in 1835 he published *Gothic Furniture in the Style of the Fifteenth Century*; this book, although the engraved designs are often unattractive and are not always consistent with Pugin's own doctrines, can be considered as the first reformist manifesto. The furniture shown is archaeologically sound and its construction openly revealed. Pugin laid great stress on integrity in design; he hated the mean, shabby and *sham* decoration which passed for Gothic among his contemporaries. He was also an advocate of nature as a basis for art and designed carved ornament and flat patterns based on natural forms which have a vigour far ahead of his time. Much of his furniture, especially when on a monumental scale, is drily archaeological and constitutes a Gothic equivalent of Salvin's Elizabethan. But some smaller pieces have a simplicity and honesty which almost conceals their Gothic origin; commercial adaptation of these simpler designs constituted an early effort to make rational furniture for the mass market. However public attention was focussed on Pugin's more elaborate designs and he was, in the end, a precursor of reform rather than a successful reformer.

Although much of the literature concerned with the decorative arts in the early Victorian period was pervaded by a self-congratulatory sense of headlong progress, many serious thinkers were extremely concerned at the general low standards of design. The consciousness that foreign designers were far superior and a reluctant recognition that an unquestioning adherence to historical styles implied a lack of invention in the present, were major factors in inspiring a movement for education in design. The commercial value of good design was insisted upon and both Parliament and manufacturers showed increasing interest in the subject. In 1837 the School of Design opened in Somerset House; provincial schools were later founded in the main manufacturing centres. Magazines such as the Art Union (1844–48), the Art Journal (1849), The Builder (1843) and the Journal of Design and Manufactures (1849–52), all took a vigorous part in the controversy surrounding the methods and administration of the Schools. They also published new designs and criticized and publicized the early provincial exhibitions of manufactures. In 1843 Prince Albert accepted the presidency of the Society of Arts which became an active

PLATE 1. Past and Present, by Augustus Egg, 1858. The first scene of Egg's morality shows a typical middle-class interior. The elegant papier-mâché chair, the 'Louis XIV' overmantle mirror, and the well-draped centre table, are all worthy of note. *Tate Gallery*.

PLATE 2. Detail of a cabinet ornamented with marquetry, gilt bronze mounts and porcelain plaques, designed by M. Eugene Prignot, and made by Messrs. Jackson and Graham for the 1855 Paris Exhibition. With its overloaded decoration and amazing technical virtuosity this cabinet is the epitome of early exhibition design, in this case by a Frenchman. *Victoria and Albert Museum.*

PLATE 3. Interior at Osborne House. Despite the fact that it is cluttered with a large number of disparate elements – balloon back chairs, 'Elizabethan' chairs, whatnots, unmatched tables and so on, this mid-Victorian interior presents a surprisingly light and elegant general effect. *Ministry of Public Building and Works.*

promoter of design. One of its members, Henry Cole, who was later, as Secretary of the Department of Practical Art at South Kensington, to lay the foundations of the Victoria and Albert Museum, tried a more direct approach. In 1848, under the pseudonym of Felix Summerly, he founded Summerly's Art-Manufactures. He persuaded well-known artists to provide designs to manufacturers and then market the products using the name Felix Summerly as a guarantee of good taste. The term 'Art-Manufactures', which Cole originated, illustrates two basic misconceptions about design which were shared by most of his contemporaries. They felt that 'Art', which amounted, in this context, to ornament, could be added in as great a quantity as needed to a 'Manufacture', in other words a basic design such as a sideboard, and that the result would be good design. The outcome, in fact, was sideboards which swayed under the weight of excessive

PLATE 4. Furniture at Osborne House. The roll-top desk and stool are based on Regency models, the harmonium and whatnot are Victorian inventions. Yet all four pieces show a restraint and functionalism typical of the best good quality conservative furniture of the mid-century. *Ministry of Public Building and Works.*

ornament. The second mistake was the belief that well-known sculptors and painters were qualified to design furniture without any knowledge of the technical side of its manufacture. However, instead of good design, they produced for the most part objects which were an uneasy amalgam of furniture and sculpture and possessed the good qualities of neither.

The 1851 Exhibition was planned by the Society of Arts and was intended as a shop-window for the best English design, presenting a direct confrontation between English and foreign furniture. Although it is now difficult to see any great difference between the two, contemporary critics felt strongly that, although cabinet work was basically sound, England lagged far behind many foreign competitors in decorative work and its design, above all France, which carried off the honours in every field of the decorative arts. The exhibits were completely unlike the normal run of furniture production; elaborate decoration and a gigantic scale were the main devices used by manufacturers to draw attention to their products. Nonetheless the exhibition provided a valuable index of popular taste in 1851; Naturalism, 'Louis XIV', and Elizabethan, mixed in varying proportions, were the dominant styles. The Mediaeval Court, which contained Gothic furniture designed by Pugin and made by J. G. Crace, was the only section to give encouragement to advocates of reform and education in design.

While the 1851 Exhibition presented a depressing picture of the progress of taste in furniture, it highlighted a sphere in which English manufacturers excelled – the use of new materials, techniques and technical devices. The Victorians were fascinated by the possibilities of technical progress and any new development received immediate publicity which the manufacturers, unlike the majority of those using more conventional methods, eagerly courted. The best known of the new materials is papier-mâché; almost exclusively centred in Birmingham, the trade had begun in the mid-eighteenth century and was at first devoted to the manufacture of trays. In the 1820s the most important firm, Jennens and Bettridge began to apply the material to furniture; they also experimented with new methods of decorating papier-mâché and their process of decorating it with pearl-shell inlay, patented in 1825, was a notable success. Papier-mâché was unsuitable as a structural material and was often mounted on a metal or wooden frame. The main articles of manufacture were small items, such as tea-caddies, pen-trays and letter racks, but chairs, tables, even a bed, were also produced, mainly by Jennens and Bettridge. Their Jenny Lind chair of 1849, Bielefeld's Albert shaving glass of 1844 and McCullum and Hodgson's table with the top painted after Landseer of 1849, are typical examples of the papier-mâché manufacturers' flair for exploiting popular public figures and artists to attract attention to their wares. However, although Jennens and Bettridge were generally respected, the design of papier-mâché articles met much criticism. A table by Turley of Birmingham shown in the Exposition there in 1849, had Tintern Abbey at the top and pinkish cupids at the bottom; it was described as 'of peculiarly vulgar design', no doubt justifiably. Metal was another material widely used for furniture. J. C. Loudon in his *Encyclopedia of Cottage, Farm and Village Architecture* (1833) recommended the use of iron in furniture. The pioneers in this field were the Coalbrookdale Iron Company of Shropshire who began in 1834 to make ornamental castings of iron. Their production was mainly devoted to hall-stands and garden furniture, displaying an immense variety of designs and great technical virtuosity but rarely a very advanced standard of design. Another important industry was the manufacture of metal bedsteads; in 1849 Messrs. Winfield, who, with Peyton and Harlow, were the leading manufacturers, were employing about 400 men in their factory in Birmingham and they continued to expand. The earlier bedsteads were comparatively crude cast iron articles but continual technical refinement allowed the production of elaborately decorated showpieces. For the mass market, however, cheapness and hygiene were the main advantages of metal and cheaper articles often possessed an elegance and simplicity which was conspicuously lacking in most other contemporary furniture.

Like papier-mâché the Derbyshire marble industry dated back to the mid-eighteenth century and was at first devoted to the production of small knick-knacks. In the early nineteenth century it was producing inlaid table tops of a rather crude type but the sudden expansion of the trade in the 1840s and 50s was due to the intervention of the Duke of Devonshire who encouraged this local industry by lending to manufacturers Florentine pietre dure models from his collection. Tables inlaid with flowers became the main article of production and were highly praised. They were, however, difficult to make and, as a result, too expensive for manufacture in great quantity. Slate, japanned to resemble marble, was used as a cheaper substitute and enjoyed some success. Novelty materials, such as coal or deers' antlers, also make an appearance in contemporary literature and a surprising number of such oddities survive. However wood was the principal material for furniture and an important aspect of the search for new materials was the wood substitute; this was usually some form of composition which could be stamped or moulded to resemble carved wood at a fraction of the expense of carver's work. Among the competitors in this field were Leake's Patent Relievo Leather Hangings, the Gutta Percha Company, Jackson's Composition, Haselden's Putty Composition and the exotically named Albano's Patent Cannabic Composition. Another means of overcoming the expense of hand-carving was the use of machinery; three main methods were used. First, an iron template could be made red hot and the 'carved' decoration burnt into the wood; the Patent Wood Carving Company were the chief users of this method although there were many other similar ventures including one in which the young Tennyson lost £500 in 1842. The second, as practised by Messrs. Wood and Co., was to stamp the ornament into the wood under great pressure. The third and most successful was the use of machinery; the most successful inventor was Thomas Jordan who in the late 1840s designed machine tools able to carve patterns of considerable complexity and which could even attempt undercutting. Nonetheless nearly all machine carving had to be finished by hand, and, despite continual efforts to find new methods or perfect old ones, conventional hand-carving survived this competition.

The search for cheap methods of carving was a reflection of the general revival of this art which took place in the 1840s. Although the historical styles demanded carved ornament, much of the credit for the prestige and popularity enjoyed by Victorian master carvers must go to W. G. Rogers, a London carver, who dominated the craft at this period. He learnt his trade during the Regency when the number of carvers in London was fast dwindling but his virtuosity, combined with good business sense, eventually won him royal patronage and a universal reputation. After his death in 1857 his two sons continued to carve and design at the top of their profession. Rogers was probably largely responsible for the keen interest which Prince Albert expressed in carving; in 1849 the latter suggested a prize for amateur carvers to be given by the Society of Arts and carving remained a genteel and aristocratic pastime until the end of the century. Professionals were able to make their reputations in the great exhibitions

PLATE 5. Detail of the 'St George' cabinet, designed by Philip Webb, and painted by William Morris, 1861. Painted decoration such as this followed the Gothic originals; it also allowed Morris and his circle, many of whom were better painters than furniture designers, to display their talents. *Victoria and Albert Museum*.

PLATE 6. Thomas Carlyle, by Mrs. Allingham, 1879. The chair, in which the philosopher sits, is typical of the mechanical chairs of various types which were produced, often under Patent, throughout the century. *Scottish National Portrait Gallery.*

and provincial schools of considerable skill emerged, devoting a large amount of their energies to the production of prestige pieces of great elaboration. In the 1862 Exhibition Thomas Tweedy of Newcastle-on-Tyne won his laurels with a Robinson Crusoe sideboard and another illustrating Shakespearean themes. His apprentice and foreman Gerrard Robinson carved the celebrated Chevy Chase sideboard, commissioned by the Duke of Northumberland, and exhibited in London in 1865. This tour-de-force ensured his reputation and he continued to work in the same vein until his death in 1890. However the most important provincial centre was Warwick. William Cookes was the first carver from that town to win fame; he achieved this with his 'Kenilworth' Buffet, an elaborate sideboard carved from an oak felled near Kenilworth Castle and decorated with scenes from Scott's novel. In 1851 it was acclaimed as 'one of the chief lions on the British side of the Crystal Palace'. His reputation was rivalled by J. M. Willcox whose pupil and successor Thomas Kendall carried on the trade until 1919, enjoying considerable royal and official patronage. Even before the influence of Ruskin and his followers began to be felt, there was a certain amount of feeling against 'the iron hand of machinery'. But the vast majority of Victorian carving has an extremely mechanical quality and those carvers who were most lionized had little influence on the

16

PLATE 7. Interior of Drawing Room, from Talbert, *Gothic Forms Applied to Furniture*, 1867. Although their scale is that of exhibition pieces, Talbert's designs show a genuine attempt to apply reformed Gothic to commercial interior design.

PLATE 8. Dante Gabriel Rossetti and Theodore Watts Dunton, by Treffry Dunn, 1882. A typical Art Furniture interior. *National Portrait Gallery*.

decoration of furniture; one of the main reasons for this was that they almost invariably applied their virtuosity to furniture forms which were becoming unfashionable. By the end of the century carving was no longer a popular method of furniture decoration.

It is ironical that the man who was most responsible for swinging public taste away from the elaborate furniture laden with carved decoration of the mid-century probably never designed any furniture himself. William Morris began as a painter and his personal talent was for the design of flat patterns for wallpaper and fabrics. His progressive ideas and practical ability led him in 1861 to found Morris, Marshall, Faulkner, and Company, described 'A company of historical artists' and to put his ideas about the decorative arts into practice. His intention was to manufacture household articles of all kinds 'in a thoroughly artistic and inexpensive manner', avoiding the mechanization and sham decoration of commercial manufacturers. The basic style of Morris and Company, as it was later known, was Gothic; indeed, with the influence of Ruskin and Pre-Raphaelitism at its height among young progressives, any other style was unthinkable, at least as a starting point. Pugin, who had designed the best Gothic furniture in the generation before, was a more specific influence. Ford Madox Brown, who had designed furniture in the 1850s which anticipated Morris's ideas, contributed painted panels to some of the 'Firm's' grander pieces, but his main achievement was in designing much of the rush-seated, green-stained seat furniture based on traditional country forms which was, unlike many of Morris and Company's productions, cheap and popular. Chairs of this type, some from Brown's designs, continued in production after the end of the century; they were also much imitated by commercial firms. This was almost the only furniture to fulfil Morris's aim of art for the masses. In sharp contrast the pieces shown by Morris and Company in 1862, although aggressively reformed and mediaevalizing, were distinctly Exhibition showpieces. Philip Webb, whose pre-1862 furniture in the Gothic style was in the Morris idiom, designed the 'St. George' cabinet, which had a simple form and owed its decorative appeal to panels painted by Morris; this return to surface ornament, as opposed to carving in deep relief, was followed by virtually all progressive designers. Painted panels were also a feature of another Morris and Co. cabinet of 1862 designed by J. P. Seddon. The Gothic whose spirit the designers working for Morris and Co. were trying to recapture was not the elegant Perpendicular, which had been the main vehicle for earlier revivalists, but the massive and unseductive style of the thirteenth century. This feeling for early Gothic was shared by two architects, William Burges and Norman Shaw, whose furniture was even more massive and uncompromising than that of Morris and Co. The 1862 Exhibition, in bringing the furniture of these reformers before a wide public, paved the way for the dissemination of their ideas and their dilution by commercial manufacturers and designers. Morris and Co.'s later furniture never repeated the originality of the earlier pieces, although the firm's designers, such as Lethaby, Jack and Benson, were extremely talented and maintained the high reputation of the firm throughout the Arts and Crafts movement.

Commercial furniture shown in the 1862 Exhibition was generally considered to represent a great advance in English design and cabinet-making skill. However, although some of the pieces were proudly stated to be 'entirely the work of English designers and artisans', foreign influence was paramount. This was reflected in the choice of the renaissance style for the most ambitious productions. Although this newly-won equality with continental manufacturers gratified those concerned with the reputation of English cabinet work, a more significant development of the 1860s was taking place in the design of standard high quality furniture. The opulent curves of the naturalistic style were replaced by rectilinear forms and carved decoration by inlaid designs which often drew their inspiration from the formalized plant-ornament pioneered by Pugin and Owen Jones. Light coloured woods with a rippling surface texture, such as walnut, hungarian ash and satinwood, became the fashion, replacing the mahogany and oak of early Victorian furniture. Regency forms seem to have formed the basis of this restrained style; major firms such as Johnstone and Jeanes, Gillows and James Lamb of Manchester, were among its practitioners. Late eighteenth century French furniture also became popular and extremely high quality reproduction pieces were produced in both France and England; Holland and Sons seem to have specialized in producing furniture inspired by this style, often incorporating marquetry panels. This rapprochement with the eighteenth century, which had been so intemperately denounced by earlier writers, met with official approval when a satinwood cabinet in the Adam style, shown by Wright and Mansfield at the 1867 Paris Exhibition, was awarded a medal. Although its superb workmanship and gigantic scale proclaim it an exhibition piece, the cabinet has a restraint and elegance far removed from the normal run of such showpieces. Henceforth furniture following eighteenth century English models was produced in large quantities by commercial firms. Sometimes these pieces were literal copies and many found their way into the early collections of Georgian furniture which were formed towards the end of the century.

The development, alongside the commercial cabinet-makers and furnishers, of a number of 'Art Furniture Manufacturers' reflected the growing influence and popularity of progressive designers. The most important figure in this movement was Bruce Talbert, a professional designer. In 1867 he published *Gothic Forms applied to Furniture*, a book much influenced by the example of Webb, Burges and Shaw. Like them Talbert tended towards a gigantic scale; he also used a basic framed construction but, instead of painted decoration, he favoured complex inlaid geometrical patterns, often combined with low relief metal or carved panels. He also introduced a vogue for bold strap hinges of a Gothic character in gilt metal. Talbert designed for Holland and Son, and for Gillows, who christened his style 'Mediaeval', as opposed to the earlier 'New Palace Westminster' Gothic of Pugin. Commercial Gothic of the 1870s strongly reflected his influence, combined with that of Burges. His second book, *Examples of Ancient and Modern Furniture*, published in 1876, advocated a rather unprogressive Jacobean style. The most influential propagandist in the battle for rational furniture was Charles Lock Eastlake, whose *Hints on Household Taste* (1868) advocated a simple, cheap and almost undecorated style. His designs had little direct influence on furniture but his book, which was often reprinted, did much to stimulate

PLATE 9. Interior scheme by Mellier & Co. for Lowther Castle, in 1872. An early and extremely interesting example of 'Free Renaissance' design; the sofa has a 'Queen Anne' character. *Carlisle Record Office.*

PLATE 10. *The First Cloud* by Sir William Quiller Orchardson, 1887. This interior is an early illustration of the neo-Georgian style, whose pallid and un-inventive tastefulness contrasts strongly with the vigour and variety of earlier Victorian design. *Tate Gallery.*

the demand for Art Furniture. The preoccupation of Eastlake and all progressive designers with mediaeval art was shared by E. W. Godwin. However he introduced a new element in about 1867 when he began to design furniture based on Japanese models. His friend, Burges, had noted the mediaeval character of the Eastern furniture shown at the 1862 Exhibition, but his monumental style had little influence on Godwin whose Japanese furniture is elegant, sophisticated, and, despite its origins in serious study, at times capricious in character – a quality one might expect from a friend of Whistler. He also used Greek vase-paintings as a basis for designs. The delicate proportions of his works were completely destroyed in the rash of commercial adaptations which catered for the Japanese craze of about 1880; in many of these motifs derived from Godwin were applied indiscriminately to European forms. Godwin himself worked extensively for the trade and the success of his style inevitably led to such debasement. Another architect, T. E. Collcutt, designed a notable cabinet for Collinson and Lock which was exhibited in 1871. This piece incorporates many of the features which were the clichés of Art Furniture for the following twenty years – ebonized wood, turned supports, bevelled glass panels, painted and inlaid ornament, and a coved top. Although much of his early furniture reflects the influence of Shaw and Talbert, Collcutt later turned to designing elaborate Renaissance pieces and thus aligned himself with the conservative side of the trade.

The self-conscious 'artiness' which characterized the Aesthetic Movement and which late Victorian satirists so much enjoyed debunking, left its mark on much Art Furniture, tending to obscure the aims and achievements of the best designers and thinkers. The main reason for this was that the trade had a virtual monopoly of the means of production and therefore commercial standards of design were all-powerful. In the 1880s, however, the ideas of Ruskin and Morris inspired a number of artists and designers to create alliances of craftsmen and artists and thus unite the fine and applied arts, ensuring high standards by producing furniture themselves. Organizing themselves into Guilds and Societies which often had strong mediaeval overtones, they made furniture which embodied their ideals of good design combined with fine craftsmanship. Its expense prevented it from reaching a wide public but it had an increasing influence on enlightened manufacturers. The first such group to be established was the Century Guild, founded in 1882 by the architect, A. H. Mackmurdo. Unlike its successors the Guild employed professional cabinet-makers to execute its designs, which were always presented as co-operative ventures and never attributed to individual members of the Guild – making it difficult to assess their contributions to the Guild's work. Mackmurdo himself was the first designer to create ornament which is indisputably Art Nouveau and the Guild's furniture often contains Art Nouveau elements. But its productions, ranging from large scale and elaborate satinwood pieces with painted, carved and inlaid decoration to a small and simple oak desk, are too disparate to be considered as a whole. The foundation of St. George's Art Society in 1883, and its successor, the Art Workers' Guild in 1884, gave an opportunity for contact and discussion between the leading artists, designers and craftsmen with progressive aims. These semi-informal associations culminated in the formation in 1888 of the Arts and Crafts Exhibition Society, which gave its name to the whole movement and brought the adjective 'arty-crafty' into the language. The Society's Exhibitions in 1888, 1889, 1890, 1893, 1896 and 1899 brought the work of most leading designers before the public and helped to give a semblance of unity to a movement which, for all the co-operative beliefs of its members, had a strong tendency towards fragmentation. The belief in a co-operative society was behind C. R. Ashbee's foundation in 1888 of the Guild and

School of Handicraft but Ashbee's furniture designs were not particularly original, unlike his remarkable Art Nouveau jewellery and metalwork. M. H. Baillie Scott also designed for the Guild but his elaborately painted pieces of simple form had a far greater influence in Germany than in this country. In fact both Ashbee and Baillie Scott produced much furniture which was international Art Nouveau in character. The Cotswold School of designers remained more faithful to the Morris tradition. This loose association originated in Kenton and Company, an Arts and Crafts venture, whose most prominent members were W. R. Lethaby and Ernest Gimson, both of whom had been trained as architects. Lethaby, who also designed for Morris and Co., produced pieces whose restraint was tempered by inlaid ornament inspired by William Morris; most were executed in unpolished oak. In 1893 Gimson, who also favoured oak, set up a workshop near Cirencester in the Cotswolds with two other former members of Kenton and Co., Ernest and Sidney Barnsley. They made plain but superbly finished furniture, often inspired by rural traditions of craftmanship, and, with their pupils and followers, perpetuated the ideas of Morris at a time when most other English designers had abandoned them. Their example had considerable influence in the earlier part of this century.

A vital part was played by English designers in the creation of European Art Nouveau. Mackmurdo, Ashbee and Baillie Scott all made important contributions but, on the Continent, C. F. A. Voysey was the most admired of all the English pioneers. His furniture designs, first executed during the early 1890s, were based on a strong belief in simplicity, fitness for purpose and the value of good craftsmanship. These ideals were shared by most designers in the Arts and Crafts movement and Voysey's use of plain and unvarnished wood was also a common feature of progressive furniture at this date. His originality lay in his use of new forms and in his subtle handling of shapes whose apparent simplicity was, in fact, highly calculated. An overtly Art Nouveau feature of many pieces was the use of elaborate metal hinges which recall his equally important work as a textile designer. Despite his European reputation Voysey retained violently insular attitudes and was unimpressed by the work of his continental followers. Furniture firms such as Liberty's, J. S. Henry and William Birch of High Wycombe, were quick to take advantage of the popularity of English design and exported large amounts of high quality Art Nouveau furniture. The strong Arts and Crafts elements which were present in most English Art Nouveau furniture are less in evidence in the work of Charles Rennie Mackintosh. His furniture is sometimes sturdy and practical but more often elegant but unfunctional. Isolated, many of his designs appear affected and eccentric but, in its original setting, Mackintosh's furniture contributed to a precarious decorative unity, elongated forms balancing the tight curves of his decorative motifs. His influence was strongest in Vienna and, although he had a following in Glasgow, most English designers dismissed him as a rather neurotic Celt. Around 1900, however, when Mackintosh was at the height of his European reputation, English progressive design was losing its impetus and the common-sense conservatism which was gaining ground precluded any understanding of Mackintosh's abstract and symbolist tendencies.

A considerable amount of commercial furniture produced after 1870 catered for fashions introduced by progressive designers; Gillow's 'Mediaeval' and popular 'Anglo-Japanese' have already been mentioned. In the 1890s many firms manufactured 'Quaint' furniture, which was a commercial caricature of Arts and Crafts design, abounding in flimsy but fanciful shapes and inlaid motifs of an Art Nouveau character, and made in cheap woods stained to resemble the unpolished oak used by Voysey and others. However these modish productions give a false impression of the generality of commercial manufactures, which, for all the variety of published designs, were mainly conservative in character. The dominant style of this period was known as 'Free Renaissance' and was based on Italian and French sixteenth-century models. The popular success of the style dated from the 1870s, although many manufacturers showed renaissance furniture in the 1862 Exhibition. In 1881 Robert Edis, a writer with little taste for progressive design, published his *Decoration and Furniture of Town Houses*, in which he advocated the Free Renaissance style. Most pieces have an abundance of shelves, brackets and cupboards in an architectural framework decorated with carved or inlaid renaissance ornament. At the very end of the century the style seems to have been overtaken in popularity by reproductions of eighteenth-century furniture. Indeed at the St. Louis Exhibition in 1904 virtually all the major British exhibits were reproductions of Georgian pieces. On the other hand the German entries were in an Art Nouveau style based on the work of English designers in the Arts and Crafts movement.

The variety and invention displayed in Victorian furniture was immense, but both progressive and traditional design lacked consistency. To attract attention by novelty for its own sake or to play safe by falling back on historical revivalism were the easiest ways of satisfying an uneducated and undiscriminating market; with a few notable exceptions, Victorian designers were unable to withstand these temptations. The periodic skirmishes between conservatives and reformers produced a number of short-lived styles but none of these combined good design with originality and, more important, lasting popularity. It is perhaps not only ironical but also appropriate that the eighteenth-century styles, so detested in the early nineteenth century, should finally have triumphed.

BIBLIOGRAPHY

This short list includes the most important studies of Victorian Furniture, all of which are essential reading for anyone taking a serious interest in the subject. They will be found to expand and supplement the necessarily compressed information in the introduction to this monograph.

Elizabeth Aslin, *19th Century English Furniture*, London (Faber & Faber), 1962.

R. W. Symonds and B. B. Whineray, *Victorian Furniture*, London (Country Life), 1962.

'Victorian Furniture', by Peter Floud. In *The Concise Encyclopedia of Antiques*, Vol. III, London (Connoisseur), 1957.

'Furniture', by Peter Floud. In *The Early Victorian Period, 1830–1860* (Connoisseur Period Guide), London (Connoisseur), 1958.

'England: 1830–1901', by Charles Handley-Read. In *World Furniture*, London (Hamlyn), 1965.

MUSEUMS AND HOUSES OPEN TO THE PUBLIC

London, The Victoria and Albert Museum; Carlyle's House; Leighton House; William Morris Gallery, Walthamstow

High Wycombe, Hughenden Manor

Isle of Wight, Osborne House

Knebworth, Knebworth House

Leicester, Newarke Houses Museum

Swaffham, Oxburgh Hall

Alnwick, Alnwick Castle

Warwick, Charlecote Park

Bangor, Penrhyn Castle

Whitchurch, Castell Goch

Details of the opening times of the museums and houses in this list, which makes no claim to completeness, can be found in *Museums and Galleries*, and *Historic Houses, Castles and Gardens* (Index Publishers). Small groups or individual pieces of Victorian furniture can be seen in many other museums and houses, and it is to be expected that, with the increasing interest in the subject, much more will be on display in the near future.

PLATE 11. A 'Drawing Room Commode' from Peter and Michael Nicholson, *The Practical Cabinet Maker*, 1826. A typical late Regency design in which the elaborate and somewhat clumsy decoration foreshadows Victorian developments.

PLATE 12. Table, burr walnut and maple with boulle-work decoration and gilt mouldings, about 1830. The elaborate decoration and simple form of this piece are typical of the best 'Grecian' furniture. *Victoria and Albert Museum*.

PLATE 13. Dining chair of carved mahogany, designed by Philip Hardwick and made by W. & C. Wilkinson for the Goldsmiths' Hall, in 1834. This sober and handsome version of the Regency klismos chair is a perfect example of the 'Grecian' style. *Worshipful Company of Goldsmiths.*

PLATE 14. Firescreen of carved and gilt wood and composition with a panel of Berlin wool-work, about 1845 to 1850. A luxuriant example of the 'Louis XIV' style. *Victoria and Albert Museum.*

PLATE 15. Chair of carved wood with Berlin wool-work upholstery, about 1845. Chairs like this one, with curvilinear outlines and 'Louis XIV' decorative detail, were produced in immense quantity and variety and form one of the basic types of the 'naturalistic' style. *Victoria and Albert Museum.*

PLATE 16. Two 'Drawing Room Couches' from Lorenzo Booth, *Original Design Book for Decorative Furniture*, 1864. A late example of the extraordinary, if undisciplined, inventiveness displayed by designers of 'naturalistic' furniture.

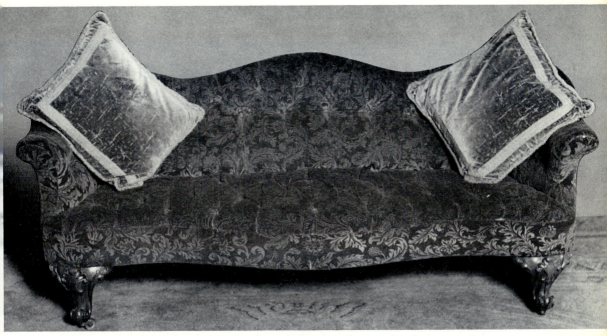

PLATE 17. Library sofa of carved walnut with velvet buttoned upholstery, about 1840. A typical, and comfortable, 'naturalistic' sofa. *National Trust, Penrhyn Castle, Bangor.*

PLATE 18. Stool of mahogany upholstered in Berlin wool-work, about 1850. This small piece shows a restraint and elegance not infrequent in mid-Victorian furniture of the less pretentious type. *Victoria and Albert Museum.*

PLATE 19. Table of mahogany with a glazed top inset with metal plaques by William Hiam of London, on a blue velvet ground, about 1850. Although the decoration of its top is unusual, this table is a good example of the type known as 'Loo Tables' (from the card-game of that name), and follows the standard pattern of three legs supporting a turned and carved column. *Victoria and Albert Museum.*

PLATE 20. Elizabethan table and chair, from Robert Bridgens, *Furniture with Candelabra and Interior Decoration*, 1838. While the table is a reasonably archaeological design, probably influenced by the illustrations in Henry Shaw's *Ancient Furniture*, 1836, the chair, despite the 'Elizabethan' decoration, is a purely Victorian design.

PLATE 21. Two chairs of tuned and carved oak, about 1840. Although their historical pedigree is dubious, 'Elizabethan' chairs of this type were one of the notable successes of Victorian historicism. *National Trust, Penrhyn Castle, Bangor*.

PLATE 22. Armchair of carved and gilded mahogany, probably designed by William Porden and made for the drawing room of Eaton Hall, Cheshire, about 1823. Despite the plentiful Gothic detail, this Regency chair is a purely fanciful creation and its design is unencumbered by any attempt at historical accuracy. *Victoria and Albert Museum.*

PLATE 23. Armchair of turned and carved ebony, with a velvet-covered squab cushion on its cane seat, about 1840. This design is probably derived from a plate in Henry Shaw's *Ancient Furniture* which shows a chair given by Charles II to Elias Ashmole. It would probably have been called 'Elizabethan', although the original is, in fact, Indo-Portuguese. *National Trust, Penrhyn Castle, Bangor.*

PLATE 24. Armchair of carved and gilded wood with velvet upholstery, about 1830. The basic dignity of this Gothic chair lends it a certain plausibility as a historicist design. However by changing the decorative details it could easily be turned into an 'Elizabethan' chair. *Victoria and Albert Museum.*

Stools

PLATE 25. Two stools, from A. W. N. Pugin, *Gothic Furniture in the Style of the 15th Century*, 1835. The lower stool, composed of roundels of Gothic tracery and carving, is in the unreformed Regency Gothic tradition, while the upper is structurally and archaeologically sound and provides an excellent example of Pugin's originality as a designer.

Pub.d April 1st 1835 by Ackermann & Co. London.

PLATE 26. Chair of oak with turned and carved ornament, about 1840. This charming and successful design is composed entirely of Gothic tracery and mouldings used in a totally un-archaeological manner. *National Trust, Penrhyn Castle, Bangor.*

PLATE 27. Cabinet, designed by A. W. N. Pugin for Abney Hall, Cheshire, about 1847. The elaborate carved decoration of this piece, true to both Gothic and nature, does not conceal its straightforward construction. *Museum and Art Gallery, Salford.*

PLATE 28. Armchair of carved oak upholstered in imitation leather, designed by
A. W. N. Pugin, for Charles Scarisbrick of Scarisbrick Hall, about 1837. The
originality of this splendid chair proves that Pugin's love of Gothic did not
confine him to the imitation of existing models. *Victoria and Albert Museum*.

PLATE 29. Table of carved walnut with inlaid decoration, designed by A. W. N. Pugin for Abney Hall, Cheshire, about 1847. The imposing and original base to this table seems unduly cumbrous, even doctrinaire, in its use of revealed Gothic construction. *Victoria and Albert Museum.*

PLATE 30. Detail of the top of the table in the preceding plate. Although the base of this table cannot be counted a total success, the decoration of the top is a triumph of Pugin's use of formalized natural forms for two-dimensional ornament.

PLATE 31. The 'Star of Brunswick' table, of carved walnut with a porcelain star let into the centre, made by Henry Eyles of Bath, for the Great Exhibition of 1851. The 'naturalistic' style here achieves a baroque vigour on the verge of toppling over into vulgarity. *Victoria and Albert Museum.*

PLATE 32. Cabinet of carved oak with brass panels and mounts, designed by A. W. N. Pugin and made by J. C. Crace for the Great Exhibition of 1851. The masterly and knowledgeable use of the 15th century Gothic style in this piece singles it out from its Exhibition competitors. *Victoria and Albert Museum.*

PLATE 33. Chair of carved and inlaid walnut with a porcelain plaque of Queen Victoria, made by Henry Eyles of Bath for the Great Exhibition of 1851. This 'naturalistic' chair achieves an appropriately feminine lightness and elegance. *Victoria and Albert Museum.*

PLATE 34. Canterbury of papier-mâché with mother-of-pearl inlay, about 1850. The production of small and elaborately decorated articles, such as this canterbury, was the chief activity of the papier-mâché industry. *Victoria and Albert Museum.*

PLATE 35. Firescreen of papier-mâché painted in various colours and set with white and green pastes, by Jennens and Bettridge, about 1850. This garish object is a splendid example of the 'Elizabethan' style misapplied. *Victoria and Albert Museum.*

PLATE 36. Sofa of papier-mâché with mother-of-pearl and painted decoration, about 1850. This piece combines a large variety of 'naturalistic' motifs into an uneasy whole, with little regard for the characteristics of the material of which it is made. *Victoria and Albert Museum.*

PLATE 37. Pedestal table of papier-mâché by Jennens and Bettridge, about 1850.
A simple and conservative 'Grecian' shape painted with highly inappropriate
decoration. *Victoria and Albert Museum.*

PLATE 38 (above). Bed of papier-mâché with brass mounts, and the original canopy, about 1850. This apparent tour-de-force in papier-mâché has in fact an iron inner structure. *Victoria and Albert Museum.*

PLATE 39 (right). Bedstead in the Renaissance style by Messrs. Winfield of Birmingham, from the *Art Journal Catalogue* of the 1851 Exhibition. A faithful reflection of wood prototypes executed with great virtuosity in brass.

PLATE 40. The Chevy Chase sideboard, carved between 1857 and 1863 by Gerrard Robinson of Newcastle. Occupying a no-man's-land between furniture and decorative sculpture, this sideboard is a superb, but none the less typical, example of this Victorian carver's work. *Trust Houses Limited, Grosvenor Hotel, Shaftesbury.*

PLATE 41. Table of oak with carved decoration, designed by Philip Webb (1831–1915), about 1865 to 1870. The 'revealed' construction of this piece recalls Pugin's most reformist work. *Victoria and Albert Museum.*

PLATE 42. Cabinet of oak painted and inlaid with various woods, designed by J. P. Seddon, and painted by Ford Madox Brown, Edward Burne-Jones, Dante Gabriel Rossetti, and William Morris, 1861. The inlaid decoration of this piece owes something to Pugin's example but the massive and uncompromising structure represents a totally new approach to Gothic. *Victoria and Albert Museum.*

PLATE 43. Cabinet, designed by Philip Webb, with doors painted by William de Morgan, about 1865. The overhanging upper part of this piece, derived from Gothic examples, was a favourite motif of designers associated with Morris.
William Morris Gallery, Walthamstow

PLATE 44. Wardrobe, designed by Philip Webb and painted by Edward Burne-Jones with a scene from Chaucer. Made as a wedding-present for William Morris, 1858–9. *Ashmolean Museum, Oxford.*

PLATE 45. Chair of turned wood, stained green, with a rush seat, made by Morris & Co. about 1865. This type of chair was developed from a traditional Sussex type and was more successful than any other types of furniture produced by the Morris 'Firm'. *Victoria and Albert Museum.*

PLATE 46. Armchair of turned and stained wood with a rush seat, designed by
D. G. Rossetti and made by Morris & Co., about 1865. A more sophisticated
derivative of the previous example. The underframe of the 'St George' cabinet
is visible in the background. *Victoria and Albert Museum.*

PLATE 47. The 'Morris' adjustable back chair, of ebonized wood with turned decoration, upholstered in the 'Bird' woollen tapestry, made by Morris & Co. from about 1866 onwards. Philip Webb designed this successful adaptation of another Sussex chair. *Victoria and Albert Museum.*

PLATE 48. Cabinet of oak with inlaid and painted decoration, designed by Richard Norman Shaw (1831–1912) and made by James Forsyth for the 1862 International Exhibition. This monumental architectural piece is the epitome of reform in furniture. *Victoria and Albert Museum.*

PLATE 49. Cradle of carved oak with gilt and painted decoration, designed by Richard Norman Shaw for one of the sons of Alfred Waterhouse, 1861. The forceful iconography – the signs of the Zodiac watching over the child – is typical of the work of such convinced gothicists as Shaw and Burges. *Victoria and Albert Museum.*

PLATE 50. Cupboard and secretaire, of painted and gilt wood, made by Harland & Fisher for the 1862 International Exhibition. Designed by William Burges (1827–81) for H. G. Yatman in 1858, and painted by E. J. Poynter. *Victoria and Albert Museum.*

PLATE 51. Wash stand, carved, painted and gilt, with mirrors, and fittings of marble and bronze, designed by William Burges for the Guest Chamber, Tower House, 1880. Burges' masterly use of polychrome and rich materials is here shown to brilliant effect. *Victoria and Albert Museum.*

PLATE 52. Cabinet of satinwood with marquetry of various woods, gilt mouldings and Wedgwood plaques, made by Wright and Mansfield for the 1867 Paris Exhibition. The superb craftsmanship and restraint of this piece contrasts equally with earlier exhibition pieces and the exuberant Gothic of reformers such as Burges. *Victoria and Albert Museum.*

PLATE 53. A library bookcase from Charles L. Eastlake, *Hints on Household Taste*, 1868. A simplified version of reformed furniture, of which Eastlake was a successful propagandist.

DRAWING ROOM IN THE LOUIS SEIZE STYLE. ✦ JAMES SHOOLBRED & COMP.Y
TOTTENHAM HOUSE, TOTTENHAM COURT ROAD, W.

PLATE 54. A drawing room in the Louis Seize style by James Shoolbred & Company. Unlike early 'Louis Seize' furniture the pieces shown in this design show a considerable knowledge of the style, albeit applied to essentially Victorian forms.

PLATE 55. Chaise-longue with deeply buttoned upholstery, about 1860. In contrast to earlier 'Naturalistic' productions, the general form of this piece is extremely restrained. *National Trust, Penrhyn Castle, Bangor.*

PLATE 56. Chiffonier of Hungarian ash with ebonized and inlaid decoration, made by James Lamb of Manchester, about 1870. An example of finely made commercial furniture, influenced both by regency models and the Art Furniture movement. *Victoria and Albert Museum.*

PLATE 57. Cabinet of walnut, carved and inlaid with various woods, with enamel plaques of birds, and metal reliefs of the 'Sleeping Beauty', designed by B. J. Talbert (1838–81), and made by Holland & Sons, 1867. Although this piece is the work of a commercial firm, Talbert, as designer, has introduced decorative motifs and constructional mannerisms based entirely on the work of reformers.
Victoria and Albert Museum.

PLATE 58. Chair of ebonized birch with carved and inlaid decoration, made by Doverston, Bird & Hull, Manchester, and probably designed by B. J. Talbert, about 1870. Strongly reformed gothic inlaid decoration is here combined with a basic shape which owes much to the 'naturalistic' balloon back chair. *Victoria and Albert Museum.*

PLATE 59. The 'Pet' sideboard, oak with carved boxwood panels, designed by
B. J. Talbert and made by Messrs. Gillow for the 1871 London International
Exhibition. The reformed gothic style is here transmogrified into an innocuous
Jacobean, acceptable both to commercial firms and exhibition visitors. *Victoria
and Albert Museum.*

PLATE 60. Sideboard of ebonized wood with silver plated fittings and inset panels of 'embossed leather' paper, made by William Watt about 1867. E. W. Godwin (1833–1886), who designed this piece, worked as an architect in Bristol in the Gothic style, but later, in London, developed an idiosyncratic style strongly influenced by Japanese art. *Victoria and Albert Museum.*

PLATE 61. Grand piano, with inlaid and gilded wood, by Marsh & Jones of Leeds. The case was probably designed by Charles Bevan, an important but obscure designer, whose work was extremely reformist in character, about 1870.
Temple Newsam House, Leeds.

PLATE 62. Chair of ebonized oak, partly turned, with an upholstered seat and back, designed by E. W. Godwin and made by William Watt, about 1880. This interesting chair is typical of Godwin's so-called Japanese style, although the legs, at least, are more influenced by examples shown on Greek vase-paintings. *Victoria and Albert Museum.*

PLATE 63. Cabinet of walnut, with Japanese carved boxwood panels and carved
ivory handles in the form of monkeys, designed by E. W. Godwin and made
by William Watt, or Collinson and Lock, about 1876. This fine piece, remini-
scent of Chinese eighteenth century furniture, was originally in Godwin's
own possession. *Victoria and Albert Museum.*

PLATE 64. Cabinet of ebonized wood with painted panels, designed by T. E. Collcutt (1840–1924), and made by Collinson and Lock for the 1871 London International Exhibition. In this cabinet, which was much admired at the time, Collcutt presented a prophetic anthology of the motifs of commercial Art Furniture. *Victoria and Albert Museum.*

PLATE 65. Cabinet of ebonized and gilt wood with stoneware plaques by George Tinworth, designed by Charles Bevan, and shown by Doulton & Co. at the 1872 London International Exhibition. Another typical example of exhibition Art Furniture, much less reformist than many of Bevan's designs. *Victoria and Albert Museum.*

PLATE 66. Sideboard of ebonized wood with incised, carved and painted decoration, probably designed by J. Moyr Smith, about 1880. The ebonized wood, multiple shelves, turned supports and painted decoration of this piece follow the pattern established by Collcutt's 1871 Cabinet. *Victoria and Albert Museum.*

PLATE 67. Chair of mahogany with painted fretwork, designed by A. H. Mackmurdo for the Century Guild, c. 1882. This chair by Mackmurdo is surprising both for the conservatism of its basic shape and for the brilliant and original early Art Nouveau decoration in the back. *William Morris Gallery, Walthamstow.*

PLATE 68. Writing desk, designed by A. H. Mackmurdo for the Century Guild, about 1886. The architectural integrity of this simple piece shows Mackmurdo at his best, in contrast to the somewhat ill-unified design of the chair shown on page 71. *William Morris Gallery, Walthamstow.*

PLATE 69. Corner cupboard of ebonized wood with incised, gilt and painted decoration, designed by Alfred Waterhouse, A.R.A. (1830–1905) and probably painted by Mrs. Waterhouse, about 1878. The painted decoration lends this otherwise unremarkable Art Furniture piece an especial charm. *Victoria and Albert Museum.*

PLATE 70. Settle of satinwood, a Century Guild piece designed in 1886 by A. H. Mackmurdo for Pownall Hall, Cheshire, and probably made by E. Goodall & Co. of Manchester. The brass repoussé panels are by Bernard Creswick and the 'Angel with a Trumpet' fabric by Herbert Horne. A fully fledged example of Century Guild co-operation, reflecting none the less Mackmurdo's strongly architectural sense of design. *Victoria and Albert Museum.*

PLATE 71. Piano of walnut and mahogany with inlay of boxwood and mother-of-pearl, designed by Alfred Waterhouse in 1882. Despite the basically Gothic inlaid decoration, the architectural framework of this piece is conservative 'Free Renaissance' in style. *Victoria and Albert Museum.*

PLATE 72. A study mantlepiece from R. W. Edis, *The Decoration and Furniture of Town Houses*, 1881. In this illustration a Morris-like turned armchair and a conservative armchair in the regency tradition stand by an overmantle in which Free Renaissance and Art Furniture motifs are intermingled.

PLATE 73. Bookcase of carved oak with gilt metal mounts and an enamelled slate top, made for John Jones by a man named Hayward, about 1870. An elaborate commercialized version of reformist Gothic. *Victoria and Albert Museum.*

PLATE 74. Bedstead of brass, made in 1890, at a cost of £600 for the visiting Edward, Prince of Wales. 'Free Renaissance' applied to brass. *National Trust, Penrhyn Castle, Bangor*.

PLATE 75. (*Page 77, above*). Sofa of mahogany, carved and inlaid with ivory, ebony and various woods, designed by Christopher Dresser (1834–1904) for Bushloe House, Leicestershire, about 1880. Dresser was a celebrated popularizer of the Japanese style in design, but was also involved, as in this piece, in the contemporary Ancient Egyptian revival. *Victoria and Albert Museum*.

PLATE 76 (*Page 77, below*). Stool of mahogany with turned decoration on the legs and a leather seat, made by Liberty & Co. about 1884. An example of Liberty's highly successful use of Ancient Egyptian models. *Victoria and Albert Museum*.

PLATE 77. Wardrobe of oak and pine with Egyptian painted decoration and tiles about 1880. This piece has an antiquarian flavour similar to the Ancient Egyptian furniture designed by Holman Hunt in the 1850s. *Victoria and Albert Museum.*

PLATE 78. Table and chairs of mahogany, inlaid with rosewood and sycamore, designed by Owen Jones (1809–74), for Eynsham Hall, Oxford, about 1872. Jones was active as a writer and designer from the mid-century until his death in 1874. His influence for the better on commercial design is exemplified by this suite, which looks far ahead of its time. *Victoria and Albert Museum.*

PLATE 79. Armchair of oak with a caned seat, made by Collier & Plucknett, of Warwick and Leamington, about 1880. A finely executed plagiarism of a design by E. W. Godwin, typical of the best 'Japanese' furniture. *Victoria and Albert Museum.*

PLATE 80. Table of oak, decorated with ebonized pegs, about 1880. High quality
Art Furniture of simple design. *Victoria and Albert Museum.*

PLATE 81. Cabinet of oak, inlaid with ebony and satinwood, with painted panels of the signs of the Zodiac by George McCulloch, designed by Lewis F. Day. This piece was shown at the first Arts and Crafts Exhibition in 1888, and its sophisticated simplicity is typical of much Arts and Crafts work. *Victoria and Albert Museum.*

PLATE 82. Cabinet of rosewood, inlaid with purplewood, tulipwood, and ebony, designed by W. A. S. Benson (1854–1924) and made by Morris & Co., about 1899. Morris & Co.'s production at the end of the century consisted mainly of high-quality Art Furniture, influenced by Arts and Crafts and Art Nouveau design, but bearing little relation to the original aims of the firm. *Victoria and Albert Museum.*

PLATE 83. Sideboard of oak inlaid with ebony, sycamore and bleached mahogany, designed by W. R. Lethaby (1857–1931) for Melsetter House, Orkneys, about 1900. An example of natural oak furniture in the best Arts and Crafts manner. *Victoria and Albert Museum.*

PLATE 84. Cabinet of mahogany inlaid with various woods, with cast brass handles, designed by George Jack (1855–1932) and made by Morris & Co. for Lady Shand, about 1900. Jack was an Arts and Crafts exhibitor and his commercial work for Morris & Co. is a somewhat glossy version of the Arts and Crafts style. *Victoria and Albert Museum.*

PLATE 85. Escritoire and stand with marquetry of sycamore and various woods, designed by George Jack, and made by Morris & Co., 1893. This piece is strongly Arts and Crafts in character. *Victoria and Albert Museum.*

PLATE 86. Chair of birchwood stained black with a caned seat, designed by George Walton (1867–1933) about 1903. Walton, a Glasgow architect, designed elegant and practical furniture, far more restrained than that of his fellow-towns-man, Mackintosh. *Victoria and Albert Museum.*

PLATE 87. Sideboard of birchwood stained black, designed by George Walton about 1903. In this well-made piece, the outer tapering legs turn outwards at a diagonal at the bottom in the same way as those of the chair by Walton, a typically elegant mannerism. *Victoria and Albert Museum.*

PLATE 88. Sideboard of oak with brass hinges, designed by C. F. A. Voysey, and made by C. F. Neilson, about 1900. The square finials of this typical Voysey piece are probably derived from Mackmurdo's designs for the Century Guild. *Victoria and Albert Museum.*

PLATE 89. Writing desk of oak with copper hinges, designed by C. F. A. Voysey (1857–1941) and made by W. H. Tingey in 1896. In this piece the two-dimensional ornament of the hinges contrasts with and complements the spatial interplay of the structure, in which the slender legs rise to serve as detached columns supporting a slender cornice, beautifully echoed in the narrow mouldings above and below the cupboard door. *Victoria and Albert Museum.*

PLATE 90. Music cabinet of mahogany inlaid with various woods, Liberty & Co., about 1897. Another typical Liberty Art Nouveau piece. *Bowes Museum*

PLATE 91. Armchair of oak upholstered in leather, designed by C. F. A. Voysey, and made about 1909 for the Essex & Suffolk Equitable Assurance Company. A few delicate curves modify the rectilinearity of this high-backed chair. *Victoria and Albert Museum.*

PLATE 92. Sofa of mahogany with inlaid ornament, upholstered in velvet, made about 1897, possibly by Liberty & Co. In this example of commercial Art Nouveau the square finials reflect the influence of Mackmurdo and Voysey, and the floral frieze that of continental Art Nouveau ornament. *Victoria and Albert Museum.*

PLATE 93. Armchair of oak inlaid with ebony, with rush panels, designed by
E. G. Pannett, and made by William Birch of High Wycombe, in 1901. This
firm were successful exporters, and this chair, of basically Arts and Crafts
design with an inlaid Art Nouveau flower, is a fine example of their work.
Victoria and Albert Museum.

PLATE 94. Chest of drawers of holly, painted green and red, designed by Ambrose Heal in 1899. This piece has a direct appeal typical of Heal's work but remarkable in commercial furniture.

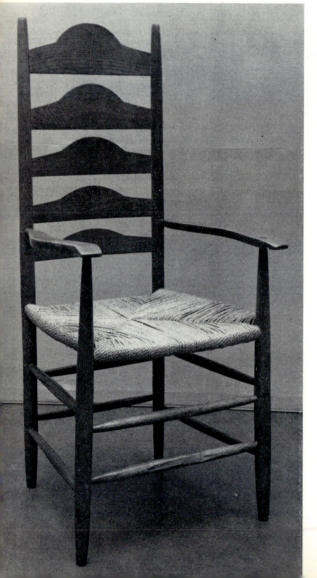

PLATE 95. Armchair of ash with a rush seat, designed by Ernest W. Gimson (1864–1919). A beautifully made and subtly proportioned Gimson version of a traditional model. *Victoria and Albert Museum.*

PLATE 96. Writing cabinet of mahogany inlaid with various woods, with steel handles, designed by Ernest W. Gimson for Kenton & Company, and shown at the 1890 Arts and Crafts Exhibition. Gimson's restraint and love of fine craftsmanship is already apparent in this early piece. *Victoria and Albert Museum.*

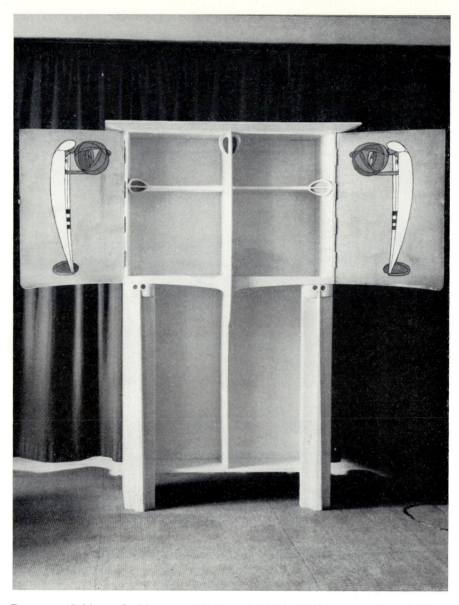

PLATE 97. Cabinet of white enamelled wood inlaid with opaque coloured glass, by C. R. Mackintosh, about 1902. A fine example of Mackintosh's mastery in balancing elongated and often asymmetrical forms. *University of Glasgow.*

Index